Leadership

A Thorough Guide To Achieving Corporate Success And Advancing One's Career, Navigating Corporate Success: Essential Strategies

(Utilizing Ethical Principles To Create An Effective And Inspiring Leadership Model)

Berndt Petz

TABLE OF CONTENT

The Development Of Future Leaders Is The Responsibility Of Current Leaders...........................1

Who Is Going To Gain From Reading This Book? 6

The Value Of Maintaining A Regular Routine.. 10

Establish Boundaries In A Way That Empowers People While Preventing Conflict.........................18

Focus On Collaboration In Addition To Your Own Personal Development:...................................23

Thinking Outside The Box 31

What Links The Gods Together 37

The Traits That Make For An Excellent Consultant..46

Mastering The Art Of Dancing With Transience 50

Enhancing Your Capabilities In The Area Of Communication In Order To Become A More Effective Leader 69

The Driven And Enthusiastic Leader 86

Intellectually Communicate With One Another. 91

Have A Perfect Understanding Of Leadership Strategies 115

How To Get Past Your Fear Of Having Panic Attacks 122

The Development Of Future Leaders Is The Responsibility Of Current Leaders.

The most effective leaders are aware that their success is gauged not just by the outcomes they produce, but also by the manner in which they foster the growth of the individuals with whom they collaborate. They make an effort to become familiar with the capabilities and limitations of each member of their team. This is done by leaders so that they can educate, coach, and mentor other people, so producing new leaders in the process.

Leaders exude such self-assurance in their own capabilities that they do not appear to be threatened when members of their teams elect to take on more responsibilities. They foster freedom and trust, believing that the task at hand will be completed without the need for excessive micromanagement.

When it comes to their work, members of teams who have strong leaders feel more powerful. They are certain that they will be treated with respect and that they will be given the opportunity to develop. This leads to an efficient team that is able to meet their deadlines while maintaining a low level of conflict. Everyone is aware that they, as individuals, contribute significantly to the success of their own teams since there are no favorites and there is an open interchange of information.

How to Develop Your Leadership Skills

Being placed in a position of authority can be a nerve-wracking experience.

Even people who have been given a great deal of training can run into problems if they are put in a leadership position. You will find some helpful advice and strategies that you may apply in order to become an efficient leader below.

Exert your ardor.

The quality that distinguishes outstanding leaders from average ones is passion. What could possibly be more exciting or motivating than working alongside someone who genuinely believes in the objectives of the organization that you are a part of? However, only having a fiery enthusiasm for anything is not going to be enough until other people can sense how much you care about the task at hand.

There are many different ways that you can demonstrate your ardour for something. Be sure to use carefully selected phrases and the suitable tone while expressing your excitement for the projects that you have to do. Get to know your employees so that they feel that you are interested in them as people and not just as workers. This will give them the impression that you care about them.

Be optimistic while discussing the initiatives that you and your team will be working on in the future. The other members of your team will be able to see that you are devoting one hundred percent of yourself to the task at hand if you let them in on your goals and strategies. When members of your team realize that you are not afraid to roll up your sleeves and get to work, it will inspire others to do the same.

Be a Good Example for Others.

One of the fundamental tenets of leadership is that a leader must provide a good example for followers to follow. You need to display the same level of motivation that you want from your staff if you want them to be productive. For instance, if you tell the members of your team that they need to report to work at the appropriate hour, then you should also be doing the same thing.

Don't carve out an exclusive loophole for yourself by making special exceptions. Even though you have a greater number of obligations than the others, if you can demonstrate that you are able to effectively manage your time, it will encourage the others to emulate your behavior.

Who Is Going To Gain From Reading This Book?

Anyone who is interested in the topic of leadership in general and leadership based on the Bible in particular will gain something from reading this book. The following set of readers will find this article to be of particular interest and benefit to them:

pastors, leaders of para-church organizations, CEOs of non-governmental organizations, and CEOs of for-profit enterprises are examples of leaders of faith-based organizations. They will gain an understanding of how to run an organization as a result of this.

members of faith-based organizations, regardless of the position they hold in those organizations.

Christian professionals who are employed by non-religious

organizations. Because of this, they will be better able to practice their faith while also being meaningful (as opposed to merely successful) in their personal life and in the business.

Students studying theology at the master's level: Institutions might recommend or prescribe this book to be used as the textbook for leadership courses inside seminaries. Many chapters of this book have already been adapted for use in leadership-related courses at the master's, master's in theology, and doctoral levels, where they have received positive feedback. This book has the potential to become a valuable resource for students taking courses in Christian Leadership within the field of Theological Education.

Anyone who has an interest in strengthening the community of the church. The phrase "preparing the bride for the bridegroom" is the central theme of this novel. It is about bringing the church back to the fundamentals of the Not-So-With-You mandate that Jesus gave, and as a result, it is abundantly prepared to assist in the formation of a church community that Jesus will be happy to return to.

Anyone who is interested in contributing to the advancement of Missions. Building long-lasting connections with people who have not yet encountered or been exposed to the gospel message is the central focus of mission work in its current form. Without the correct relationships in place, missions cannot be successful. This book will assist those who consider themselves to be "missionaries" in cultivating the correct behavior that will encourage others to want to relate to you and listen to the Gospel message that you are sharing.

The Value Of Maintaining A Regular Routine

One of those qualities that does not pay off in the near term is consistency. But it does pay off in the long term. Maintaining consistency can be challenging because there are times when it would be simpler to find alternative answers to the majority of difficulties.

But as I often say, everything that seems to lead to an immediate advantage eventually leads to a problem that is much larger and more difficult to manage in the future. This is something that I have found to be true time and time again.

If you tell a lie in order to address an issue in the short term, you might be able to get away with it, but in the long run, your relationships with your employees will suffer, and they won't have any faith in your ability to lead.

"Integrity is without a doubt the most important attribute for a person in a leadership position.

Without it, there is no real chance of success, regardless of whether one is working on a section gang, playing on a football field, serving in the armed forces, or working in an office.

(The General Dwight David Eisenhower)

Being consistent calls for making sacrifices; it necessitates confronting problems head-on as they emerge, without putting things off or trying to find workarounds or repeatedly putting "patches" in place. Being consistent also calls for having the courage to take risks.

"If no one hates you, means you're by doing something wrong."

You can't make everyone happy all of the time! If you are successful in satisfying everyone, it indicates that you do not take consistent positions and that, in an awkward attempt to please everyone, you are not managing your resources to the best of your ability. In addition, if you are successful in pleasing everyone, it indicates that you are not taking consistent stances.

"Don't follow the crowd but let the crowd to follow you"

(Prime Minister Margaret Thatcher)

Always be the embodiment of the ideals that you believe in, and never preach something that you don't practice yourself.

It is inappropriate to pretend that there is nothing wrong with something in order to avoid having a conversation about it; instead, it is appropriate to point out the problem and make it known. Problems that are avoided will rear their ugly heads at the most inopportune times, and when they do, you won't be able to keep your feelings in check. You could lash out and criticize previous events just to let some steam off, but you'll likely come to regret it later. Therefore, despite the fact that it may be challenging, it is best to confront issues when you are composed and have your wits about you.

A good rule of thumb to follow in life and business alike is to avoid making commitments if there is any doubt that you will be able to follow through on them. If you are not in a position to fulfill your promises of promotions, individual awards, or any other perks, do not make those promises. This is due to the fact that any business choice could be subject to alter up until the very last day until a promotion is made public. Because of this, it is in your best interest to exercise extreme caution because the disappointment caused by a broken promise is never easy to get over and has the potential to badly damage your relationship with your employees.

Sometimes, the most important thing is not to make the correct decision or the wrong decision, but rather to make a decision that is consistent with our values and what we have consistently communicated to our people.

It is preferable to err honestly than to make a decision that could have been better but would have been detrimental to your team's performance.

It is also easier to avoid partiality when you are consistent. Everyone has their own tastes, and it is unavoidable that our staff will have both loves and dislikes.

This indicates that there are some people who we will get along well with right away, while there are others who we will find it difficult to simply have a cup of coffee with. A competent manager needs to be able to keep their personal life and company life separate, and they should endeavor to treat all of their employees in an equitable manner.

It is frequently difficult since it takes a great lot of work to conceal your dissatisfaction from a person that you do not tolerate. This makes the situation more difficult. In this situation, you should make an effort to evaluate only the quality of the work that was done and not the person who carried it out; otherwise, you run the risk of losing your ability to be objective. If we don't like a person, he or she can carry out a hundred activities perfectly, but at the first mistake, even a minor one, we will be ready to point it out and criticize them.

On the other hand, when it comes to a person with whom we have developed a positive relationship, we will do the complete opposite: we will force that person to look beyond each and every imperfection and concentrate on the lone action that was carried out successfully.

When it comes to our brain's unconscious processes, we need to use extreme caution. Always make an effort to take an objective stance when evaluating the work of your collaborators.

We will be able to avoid the appearance of bias and move in the correct path in our pursuit of respect and esteem as a result of this.

It is important to keep in mind that our primary purpose at work is to perform our jobs; we are not being compensated to win favor or form friendships with coworkers, particularly with managers and subordinates.

Establish Boundaries In A Way That Empowers People While Preventing Conflict

You may be familiar with the account of Moses that is contained in the Old Testament of the Holy Bible.

Moses was in charge of more than a million Israelites at one point. It was expected of him to act as the judge in any and all cases, whether civil or criminal.

It goes without saying that this had a negative impact on his health and came dangerously close to taking his life.

Thankfully, his father-in-law Jethro intervened and put an end to the craziness that was going on.

"Moses, please stop doing that; it's not a good thing. You have no choice but to seek assistance with this matter. Go out and find some decent guys in each tribe, and while you focus on the more important issues, let them worry about the details of the smaller problems.

Moses gave it some serious thinking. However, he did require some sort of release. Because he was exhausted, he came to the conclusion that Jethro could very well be onto something.

Are You Prepared to Let Go of It?

When you are in control of something, it is easy to get the feeling that you need to make all of the decisions for your organization.

However, you are well aware that this is impossible. In addition to that, you do not wish to be distracted with the insignificant matters.

It's possible that Moses experienced the same thing.

Do any of these factors get in the way of you achieving your goals?

It's possible that you take pleasure in the sense of superiority that comes from commanding the actions of others. Or perhaps you simply do not put your faith in the judgment of others for anything more significant than petty disagreements. It's possible that you feel like a bad person for allowing someone else take responsibility for something that you should be handling yourself.

You need to establish some boundaries unless you want to find yourself constantly overworked, irritated, and fatigued in the future.

How to Establish Boundaries in a Way That Gives People Agency While Also Preventing Conflict

In your company, decisions are being made constantly by a variety of different people.

They have any idea what sort to create, do they?

If you establish some limits for them, they will.

Everyone ought to be aware of what it is that she is accountable for.

Everyone ought to be aware of the kinds of interactions that are appropriate with their coworkers, customers, and the leadership of the firm.

And everyone ought to be aware of what the expectations are of him.

Do not make the assumption that people are aware of these facts. Involve them again. Put it in writing and store it in a place where you can find it readily. Maintain access to it in the event that a question or disagreement arises.

In addition to this, maintain the ability to adjust the guidelines in the event that something unexpected comes up.

Your people need to be informed about the kinds of choices that are appropriate for them to make on their own. Also, while making a choice that is outside of one's scope of authority, there should be a procedure in place where the individual in question can offer a suggestion to you. Naturally, as the leader, the choice rests solely in your hands in the end. However, delegating some of the burden for thinking it through to them might save you a lot of time, particularly in the event that the concept proves to be a good one.

Focus On Collaboration In Addition To Your Own Personal Development:

The ability to foster growth not only in oneself but also in one's followers and in those with whom one comes into contact is one of the most important qualities of an effective leader. If you are just an average person but you give people positive reinforcement, then you are the one who has the potential to steer other people toward achievement, and you have the potential to become a leader.

The average person may have some egotistical tendencies; this explains why they are more prone to think about themselves than about other average individuals or their own team. On the other hand, if you are just an average person who doesn't just think about themselves but also about the people they work with, then you are already a leader, or at the very least, you have the potential to become a leader.

Always Look on the Bright Side:

If you are able to maintain a good attitude at all times and also inspire positivity in those around you, then you are the leader, even if others consider you to be no more than an average person. A genuine leader will always possess the ability to maintain a positive attitude, even in challenging situations where the majority of people struggle to do so. You are a leader if you have the ability to influence your teammates even in the most difficult situations, when the pressure of the circumstances would cause an average person to crumble under the weight of the demands placed upon them.

It is possible to deduce from this that the traits you already possess, rather than the strength of what was written down in advance, are what will determine whether or not you become a true leader. If you still believe that you can become a leader just by virtue of God's writing and not by virtue of your own talents, then you need to follow the paths that have been given above to become a leader from what you are. If you do not believe that you can become a leader by virtue of your own skills, then you need to follow these paths. You can also be the one who thinks positively and makes everyone around you think positively; then you have the quality of a great leader since you are the one who makes everyone else think positively. You only need to have the bravery to stand by the people or the team that is in need of a leader, and then you will be anointed as the leader of the group that is in need of a leader.

It is therefore possible to say that a great leader can be produced from an ordinary guy just by virtue of the excellent skills and attitude that the individual possesses, and not by what was written on the individual's palm or on the forehead.

Taking Ownership and Responsibility

"Great leaders accept responsibility, while immoral leaders point the finger of blame at others."

It is common practice for those in leadership positions to assign blame. When things don't go as planned, people are quick to point fingers and single out the person or object that they believe was to blame for the debacle. This is the path of least resistance. It is far simpler to point the finger at someone else and assign responsibility. Be conscious of the fact that this is detrimental to the efforts you are making to position yourself as a leader, as well as to everyone else. Because of this, the person who is being blamed will feel as though they can no longer trust you, which, as we will see in the following paragraphs, can have a negative impact on your ability to build trust. If we place responsibility on the process, the person who was responsible for developing the process would feel as though they have been deceived. What does the act of assigning blame signify? It shows that the leader wasn't as prepared as they may have been for the situation as a whole. Just give that some thought for a second. When you point a finger at somebody, there are three fingers pointing back at you at the very moment that you do so. Instead of pointing fingers, take responsibility for your actions. When faced with a challenge, a responsible leader will declare, "I am the one who must make it happen." The team's leader will spend some time in advance preparing and analyzing the group's requirements. This can be seen through the individual's activities in a number of different ways.

The leader is accountable for the team's deeds, regardless of how positive or negative they may be. We are all aware of the weaknesses that exist inside the group and have devised strategies to overcome the challenges that we face. No one is to be held responsible for the failure of any initiatives. When leading a team, leaders will move up from the "just one of the team" position to the "leader" position by assuming responsibility for determining the group's goals and objectives and communicating those to the members. This is demonstrated by the fact that they are no longer a part of the team. You no longer engage in social activities outside of work, such as lunches or other get-togethers with coworkers. You step up to take care of the problems and eliminate the obstructions. Leaders treat everyone with respect and maintain their integrity while doing so. It is possible to get anything by being proactive and taking responsibility for your actions. You will get the chance to demonstrate our capabilities thanks to this offer. If we take responsibility for what happened, we will have the opportunity to demonstrate how we can remain calm and collected in the face of adversity or while working through a crisis. Your team, the initiatives you're working on, and the reputation you have as a leader will all advance as a result of this. You will see a shift in the mentality of your team as it pertains to embracing responsibility and accountability when you demonstrate these traits through your own actions. The members of your team take responsibility for the outcomes. They understand that they are responsible for their own conduct as well as the work that they do and accept that responsibility. The spirit of collaboration is fostered, and the team's performance is elevated as a result. You have matured both as a leader and as a member of the team thanks to your management.

Thinking Outside The Box

The majority of people who are going through emotional upheaval choose to express themselves creatively rather than having a conversation with another person and revealing their feelings. It might be anything from painting to crafting antiques to writing a wonderful poem or anything else you can think of. A person who is experiencing emotional turmoil can start to feel better and more relaxed by engaging in creative activities like these. It is a form of catharsis for them to experience it.

Analysis and Reflection

When you actively listen to someone, you are paying attention to what is being said in its purest form. Active listening engages your brain in a different manner than passive listening does, even if it is not always necessary to have a reaction to what the other person is saying you. Concentrate on just taking in what is being said rather than drawing hasty judgments or feeling as though you are obligated to concur with an opinion that is being expressed. Pay attention not only to the words that are being spoken but also to the message that is not being spoken. Observe the individual's posture, eyes, and facial expression. You can learn a lot about how the person genuinely feels about the topic by paying attention to these indications. When it comes to topics that are particularly difficult to articulate, the words themselves may not be able to convey the entire extent of the sentiments.

One instance of this is when a buddy tells you that they are doing well even if you are aware that they are going through a challenging moment. You may see that they are teary-eyed and shaky as a result of the weight of what they are going through, even though the words that they speak may represent this sentiment. If your friend ever needs your help, all they have to do is ask, and if you are a good listener, you will be able to give it to them. If you pay careful attention to the indications that are being offered, a simple promise of support may be all that is needed to completely change the course of their day. You might have missed these indications and went on as if nothing was wrong if you had been passively listening to the situation instead of active listening. Your friend might have gotten the impression as a result that you do not care about them at all.

When there is a problem that needs to be solved, an active listener will figure out a way to chime in and give a solution when the opportunity presents itself. If you pay close attention to the specifics that are being communicated, it will be simple for you to think of potential solutions to the issue that has been presented to you. There are a lot of people who are under the impression that they are unable to communicate with other people, while in fact, the skill that needs to be worked on the most is listening. When you pay attention to what other people are saying, generating talking points will become much simpler for you because there will already be ideas for you to explore. Having this kind of participation in talks facilitated for you can do a lot to build your self-confidence. Your ability to speak and listen will grow easier for you to handle as you increase the amount of time you spend participating in activities.

You can keep your mind in tip-top shape by making active listening a regular part of your routine. Because your entire brain is actively participating in the dialogue that you are having, you can be certain that you are exercising both your capacity for empathy and your capacity for critical thinking. Because of the distinct expectations placed on passive listening, this does not occur. You can become a part of a high-engagement experience that will allow you to develop as a person if you maintain awareness of the conversation at all times and stay on top of the latest developments.

When you chat to someone else in the near future, you should make sure that you are engaging your active listening abilities. You will most likely discover that it is much simpler for you to identify with the person in question, as well as that you have a better understanding of what it is that you ought to say to them. This puts you in a situation where you can think about and examine fresh ideas and thoughts. When you listen to the experiences and perspectives of other people, you might frequently find new avenues of interest that you might wish to investigate in the future. If you are an active listener, you will accrue a significant number of benefits throughout the course of your life. Even if you discover that the majority of the time, you simply take in information without actively participating in the listening process, there are ways in which you can improve your skills.

Enter each interaction with the mindset that the person talking to you has something worthwhile to teach you and you can learn from them. Pay close attention to what they have to say and refrain from forming any snap conclusions or offering any ideas before doing so. Wait until they have finished expressing themselves before adding your two cents to the conversation. If a solution is being sought, you should make an effort to take the words that were provided to you and combine them with all of the non-verbal indicators in order to formulate a response that is empathic and understands the other person's perspective. As soon as you have this mastered, active listening will be something that comes naturally to you.

What Links The Gods Together

Let's hear about the connections amongst the demigods. According to the bhakti writings, whenever there was anarchy or upheaval in the universe, the gods of the underworld would make their way to the Ocean of Milk in order to commune with Lord Vishnu. They would communicate their wants and desires to him through their hearts while meditating on him while seated on the banks. The power of his response would be transmitted with great deliberation through the heart. He had an understanding of their emotions, and they had an appreciation for his reactions. Mantras were the only words that were uttered. The connection was one that went straight to the person's heart. They had a profound understanding that in order to solve any problem, all they needed to do was speak via their hearts, which is where the solutions would also appear. They were granted the authority to handle the myriad of obligations that were required of demigods as a result of this security.

I will instruct you on how to communicate with your child in a way that is empathic so that you may form a heart-to-heart relationship with them. We are moving up to Level 3, which is represented by the letter "P" in the word "EMPOWERMENT."

Protect Their Emotions is the objective of Level 3.

Hearing is the very first stage in the process of connecting with someone or anything. That is, at its core, the way in which we establish a connection with the hearts of our children. We are able to hear them: the words they say, the feelings they experience, and the concepts that they communicate, all of this must first be strengthened. Your child will develop a greater sense of confidence in their capacity to interact with people if you demonstrate to them on a daily basis that the emotions that are going on inside of their chests are genuine, significant, and deserving of attention.

After we have given them the opportunity to relate to us and have listened to their feelings, the underlying needs that they have become apparent. They will become more powerful as a result of our efforts to protect their hearts.

When we listen to our children's emotions, we are communicating to them that "I see you and I accept you."

My heart will always be open to your heart.

You're familiar with the scene in the movie Avatar where the giant blue animals communicate with the other species by using their tails, right? After they have successfully fused their tails together, they gaze deeply into one other's eyes and whisper, "I see you."

You will accomplish this goal by repeatedly providing our child with an accurate and attentive listening experience. You will be telling them, in a profound and profoundly interior manner, "you are worthy."

Now, you might believe that you have already heard your child, and you might spend an interminable amount of time listening to their wailing and complaining. This process is going to be strengthened by the fact that we are going to listen to them in such a way that they may learn to solve their own problems, and we are also going to provide them with precise phrases to assist them in doing so. However, the first step is to just listen to what they have to say. Hearing does not entail listening to someone and then offering them advice. There is a wide variety of compassion training available online in the form of programs. I'll start with a straightforward example here.

The procedure is as follows.

MAINTAINING CONTROL OF ANGER

Do I still feel rage sometimes? Of course I do; after all, I am a human being. But I've discovered that relying on God to help me regulate my responses is the best strategy. In the book of Ephesians chapter 4, verses 26 and 27, it says, "Be angry, and do not sin: do not let the sun go down on your wrath, nor give place to the devil." God gave each of us the capacity to feel anger, and the sinful act is not the anger itself but how we respond to it when it arises. For instance, when I hear about a crime or an injustice, it makes me really indignant. However, rather than forming a group of vigilantes and taking matters into my own hands, I will have to rely on law enforcement and the judicial system to resolve such concerns rather than taking matters into my own hands.

What exactly sets off your temper and makes you angry? Is it the individual who is following too closely behind you in traffic, or is it the neighbor's raucous party? Does it happen when you are hungry and weary at the same time? Do you find yourself frustrated when a subordinate has been given instructions to complete a task, but the task is not completed? It's possible that the worker is the one curious about the rationale behind a requirement that something be done in a specific way. It's possible that you don't enjoy being questioned, and that you want absolute loyalty from the soldiers under your command.

There are at least a hundred different situations that have the potential to make us angry; the question is, how do we respond when we find ourselves in these predicaments? Several years ago, I knew a man by the name of Explosive Eddie who worked as a driver for a tractor-trailer company that supplied gasoline and diesel fuel to local gas stations. When Explosive Eddie witnessed other individuals engaging in behavior that he believed put them in danger, he confronted them in a furious manner. When you're behind the wheel of a truck carrying nine thousand gallons of flammable liquid, you definitely want the man who is smoking ten feet away to put out his cigarette before a fire breaks out. Nevertheless, how we react to the circumstance influences how the other person responds to it. For instance, if Explosive Eddie had asked the man, "Sir, would you mind putting out your cigarette?", the man could have been persuaded to comply. This gasoline is highly combustible, and if there is a fire, it may potentially take both of our lives. It is quite possible that the person smoking the cigarette will snuff it out since he does not want to perish in a raging inferno of flames. On the other hand, Explosive Eddie's go-to response was always something along the lines of "Hey, you idiot jerk! What the heck are you trying to pull!? Assassinate us! Huh!?" How do you think you would respond if someone yelled at you in that manner? Explosive Eddie frequently shared with me the stories of the times he yelled at his employer or verbally assaulted him. When I conveyed my surprise that Eddie's employer let him get away with his actions, Eddie was truly taken aback. Guess what happened: Explosive Eddie's supervisor became fed up with his constant outbursts and finally fired him as a result.

The Traits That Make For An Excellent Consultant

There is a long list of characteristics that define a great consultant, however the following five are absolutely necessary to reach the pinnacle of the profession:

Respect for Professionalism: When working with clients, consultants should always bear in mind that they should maintain a professional level of interaction with them. There are instances when it is simple for internal consultants to adopt a "employee" frame of mind. However, this strategy might backfire in many contexts since it prevents others from viewing you as an outsider to the problem that you were attempting to solve. In point of fact, some businesses discover that they are paying external consultants not only to provide the same advise as the internal consultant, but also for a halo effect, which is an appearance of increased authority established simply by the fact that they have an outsider's perspective: To put it another way, a perspective that is thought to be more objective.

Participant in a team: Consultants are expected to demonstrate that they are participants in a team, that they are open to learn, and that they sincerely value the input and knowledge of other people. It is essential to cultivate productive working relationships with one's contemporaries.

When faced with a challenge, consultants are expected to use sound judgment and refrain from making hasty inferences or assumptions about the nature of the issue. Before making a choice, they need to carefully mull over the information at hand, seek input from their colleagues and consult with management.

Skill in communication: consultants need to be able to communicate effectively both orally and in writing. Since you are frequently considered to be the subject matter expert, you should be able to articulate your thoughts in a clear and convincing manner.

A capacity for attentive listening: consultants will encounter a wide variety of clients, each of whom possesses their own set of distinguishing features. You will be as well. You should train yourself to have outstanding listening skills and you should encourage everyone around you to talk freely. This results in a greater sharing of information, which, ultimately, can make the process of recruiting candidates more streamlined and efficient.

A solid understanding of one's obligations It is essential for internal consultants to have a solid understanding of the responsibilities associated with their function, in addition to the practices and parameters of the role.

You may find that each customer has a unique understanding of the responsibilities associated with the work of a consultant. Before beginning any further work for a client, a recruiter acting in the capacity of consultant should make it a point to get a clear understanding of the deliverables and expectations of that client.

Mastering The Art Of Dancing With Transience

When I was younger, I placed a high priority on being liked and accepted by others. We used to recite the well-known prayer, "God grant me the serenity to accept the things I cannot change, the courage to change the things I can change, and the wisdom to know the difference," as part of the recovery program I used to attend for alcoholism and addiction, which I am fortunate to have started and continued using for many years.

The work that I completed with my personal coach, Steve Hardison, brought this deserving petition one step closer to being answered. I've learned to welcome the things I can't alter, and I teach my clients how to do the same. Rather than merely accepting the things I can't change (and these days there are a lot of them), I've learned to welcome them.

A simple act of "acceptance" may give the impression (to the ego, which is desperately attempting to cling to stability) that change is an unwanted incursion, something that must be stoically endured until "normal" returns. When we were young children, we couldn't help but approach everything with genuine interest and fascination; but, if we consistently keep these two creative queries alive — "What's good about this?" and "How can I use it?" — curiosity can be rekindled, just as it was when we couldn't help but approach everything with genuine interest and excitement.

Where is the opportunity hidden within this so-called problem? should become a standard question asked during the majority of coaching sessions.

"Yes, we are able to fashion the setting!"

Werner Erhard, a renowned professor of leadership, is credited with coining the phrase "Context is decisive." because the context of any given circumstance is up to us to construct inside it. The vast majority of people either do not see that or do not even want to see it. They have the mindset that the context is an inherent restriction that comes with every circumstance, and there is nothing they can do to change that. When someone brings up a recent change, people typically respond with either "Oh, wow, that's terrible!" or "Hey, that's pretty cool." Consisting of! There is a consensus among us! But is that a requirement? Instead, we may make it happen by approaching it from the perspective of possibilities.

This is an example of context creation that I utilized for the coaches in my coaching school who were freaking out about their livelihoods when COVID-19 spread all over the world. "I'm afraid that as a result of the pandemic and the restrictions it imposes, my prospective customers will have a reduced likelihood of hiring me."

Not at all; in fact, just the reverse! People who were confined to their houses, did not have to travel, and were not otherwise engaged in a variety of personal and professional activities had more time to be coached over the phone or via Zoom. Not only that, but they had more opportunities to spend time alone, which allowed them to engage in self-reflection and consider how they might prefer their professional lives and personal relationships to be.

In addition, the lockdowns and limits reduced the amount of face-to-face interaction. It was revealed, however, that people have a deep-seated desire to engage in conversation with one another. They were more receptive than at any other time in the past to the idea of having a life coach or a business coach (who should be the same thing) who they could talk to on a regular basis.

The coaches who were afraid and seeking to just "accept" what they thought to be an entirely terrible circumstance changed their approach to the game by being more hesitant and apologetic about their job. They went so far as to lower their prices in an attempt to attract customers they presumptively believed would not be interested in receiving coaching during that difficult period, particularly if it was not provided in person.

Those coaches, on the other hand, who were open to this shift in circumstances and saw it as a sign that prospective customers desired and required their assistance more than ever before were successful in growing their businesses. The majority of the instructors I was collaborating with consistently said, "I've just had my best month ever."

This is not to deny or minimize the enormous amount of pain that COVID-19 caused. Instead of going into hiding and playing the part of a victim, it is always more creative and powerful to look for possibilities to help people and the world rather than accepting the role of a victim. This is because when my dedication remains steadfast to serve people and the world, I want to build a sustainable career doing so.

Proceed with action

Imagine that you are an exceptionally capable student. Fill in the blanks in the text that follows in your action guide to get started on developing your new identity. Produce anything between five and ten statements.

I am an inexorable student, and for that reason I...

B. Have a mentality that is open to growth

You aren't merely perpetuating a fiction or something you tell yourself to feel better about yourself when you state that you're a learner. Altering one's mental approach to learning (i.e. shifting from a fixed mindset to a growth mindset) has been found to improve one's ability to learn and retain new information.

Carol Dweck's book "Mindset" is largely responsible for the widespread dissemination of the idea of a development mindset. Having a growth mindset implies acknowledging that you are capable of personal improvement and adjusting your behavior accordingly. It's coming to terms with the fact that your capabilities aren't static and that you aren't bound to remain in the same place for the rest of your life just because of where you are right now. People who have a growth mindset have a strong desire to learn new things and the belief that their intelligence can be improved through time. As a consequence of this, they will frequently:

Take on the problems before you. They are wise to the fact that overcoming obstacles is the only way to progress in life. As a consequence of this, individuals are excited by the prospect of taking on new tasks and have faith in their capacity to solve problems.

Continue forth despite the difficulties you face. They are well aware that in order to achieve their objectives, they will have to put in a lot of effort and will face a lot of challenges along the way. The only option is to go through it. They are aware that the road they need to take involves being truthful with themselves and confronting their shortcomings.

Consider your efforts to be a means to achieve mastery. They believe that making an effort is required in order for them to advance toward mastery. They are aware that achieving success is a multi-stage process that includes both highs and lows along the way. It is impossible to avoid experiencing failures and letdowns.

Take into account any suggestions for improvement. Everyone has shortcomings and areas of blind spot that they need to recognize and work on improving. It is essential to be open to receiving constructive comments and, perhaps more crucially, to act on that critique, despite the fact that doing so may seem awkward. People that have a growth mentality are open to receiving feedback in the form of constructive criticism. This is one of the most powerful tools that individuals can employ if they wish to advance in their field.

Gain wisdom from the achievements of other people. Even though they may experience feelings of envy at times when they see the success of other people around them, in the end, they are resolved to get as much knowledge as they can from others who have achieved great things. They are willing to put aside their pride and search for ways to do better. They engage in activities such as questioning, returning to the basics, taking more classes, and many others. They continue to get better with time. They prioritize getting better at whatever they do.

Never try to reveal a secret from the past of a person you are currently engaged with in view of future possibilities (personal or professional), from the person's past if you got it somehow, because once the guarded secret surfaces, insecurities deepen and, the currently ongoing relationship with a promising future vanishes! Never try to reveal a secret from the past of a person you are currently engaged with in view of future possibilities (personal or professional) from the past! The reality is that everyone harbors some secrets, whether at the individual level, in relation to corporate affairs, or in relation to loss and profit modules. These secrets should not be revealed under any circumstances because doing so may alter cognitive decision making and disrupt ongoing integration between two business entities or associated partners. In a nutshell, we are able to draw the following conclusions about what it means to do pure business: commercial transactions on business terms and negotiation possibilities; maintaining a business focus; and avoiding anything to do with the painful past. Therefore, this component of employee behavior must to be monitored in order to maintain a positive work culture, and training procedures ought to be designed taking into consideration this context.

From a psychological point of view, a secret is connected to an experience from the past, and it is either retained as a treasure (if the secret is good and positive), or as a healed wound (if the secret is bad and negative). In the event that the good secret is revealed, one feels betrayed (as the treasure is lost), and in the event that the terrible secret is revealed, one feels broken (the old wound bleeds again)! In both instances, a person's mental state becomes cognitively warped, and as a result, disintegration can be witnessed in the context of the person's communication style and decision-making process. The disintegration generates alienation from the current connection status, which points towards a division; as a result, no professional transaction can be fixed using this method. In order to have sufficient leverage in business talks, the personnel of any firm should always be trained in accordance with this psychological element. This is necessary in order to achieve sufficient leverage.

BUSINESS LESSON: If you want to develop a fresh partnership, you shouldn't reopen old wounds, even if you already know some secrets that are unrelated to the continuing business agreement. In order to reach a resolution, we should keep them under control.

Developing your charisma and expanding your personal influence

There are a lot of different ways to improve people's perceptions of your charisma and your personal effect, but in this article I'm only going to talk about strategies that don't require any money and can be used right away. We all get into poor patterns of behavior over time, and we have to make a conscious effort to rein ourselves in if we want to ensure that we are making the most of both ourselves and the circumstances in which we find ourselves. Your resourcefulness is a significant contributor to your charm, and you need to make the most of what you have while avoiding feelings of inadequacy.

Taking in Air

When you speak, make an effort to take slow, deep breaths that come from the lower part of your lungs. Because of this, the tone will be able to sound more full and confident, and you will have greater control over the volume.

Garments with the appropriate fit

Do not undervalue the importance of wearing clothes that fit properly. I know this may sound like stating the obvious, but we all know people who dress in a way that they consider to be fashionable but that other people consider to be improper. Do not act in this manner! In settings that are more formal or professional, it is expected that one will dress conservatively and in garments that fit appropriately. The power of a well-fitting suit cannot be overstated.

Standing stance

Your posture has an effect on a variety of factors, not just how other people see you. A healthy and correct posture will make it possible to work more effectively, resulting in less fatigue for the body, and will also significantly improve the quality of the voice. Be aware of your posture at all times because poor habits are so readily formed. Pull yourself up by your bootstraps and sit up straight!

Sound Waves

The voice is the most malleable tool at your disposal, and you should approach it as though it were. The easiest method to portray confidence and charisma is through the use of your own voice. If you want to improve your delivery, it would be a good idea to listen to prominent speakers like Anthony Robbins and pay special attention to stand-up comedians. In order to enhance the quality of your speaking voice, the following are some suggestions that you may put into practice right away:

Try contracting your abdominal muscles when you talk; this will assist you in projecting your voice from your diaphragm.

Although you may choose to tighten your abdominal muscles and lower back in order to improve the quality of your voice, the rest of your body should be as relaxed as is humanly possible.

If you are standing, arrange your feet such that one is slightly in front of the other and shift your weight forward so that you are standing tall.

You should move your shoulders down in order to straighten your back and lift your head, keeping your chin parallel to the ground and neither lowered nor raised. This will help you straighten your back and lift your head.

Enhancing Your Capabilities In The Area Of Communication In Order To Become A More Effective Leader

We frequently find ourselves in positions of leadership in a variety of settings and contexts. This includes leadership at the family level, as well as leadership at the organizational level and the national level. The desire to be a better leader comes easily to anyone who finds themselves in a position of authority, regardless of the level at which they find themselves. Despite this, there aren't too many people who have managed to be successful in this area. The inability of leaders to effectively communicate with their followers is one of the crucial tools that brings down the effectiveness of leadership.

The exchange of information between individuals is accomplished through a process known as communication. It was either expressive or receptive at the same time. The growth of both your professional and personal lives depends heavily on your ability to communicate clearly and fluently. It is also essential to the process of achieving greatness in leadership. Therefore, everyone who aspires to achieve leadership excellence should make it a priority to cultivate a mindset that prioritizes clear and effective communication, and they should make it a point to consistently improve on the art of leadership communication even before they achieve any degree of leadership position. By properly motivating and inspiring their people, good leaders are able to effectively communicate with them. In addition, the most successful businesses make communication both clear and efficient in order to foster a culture of discipline, accountability, and strategic alignment.

Communication is Comprised of Three Elements: the Verbal Message (the Words We Choose), the Para-Verbal Messages (How We Say the Words), and the Nonverbal Messages (Our Body Language). Messages that are lucid and to the point can be transmitted with the help of these three components. In addition to this, we rely on them to successfully receive and interpret the messages that are given to us. It is common for there to be confusion when the verbal component, for example, states "yes," but the non-verbal component reveals "no." In order to communicate well, one needs to coordinate the three components of communication such that they accurately depict the message that is being conveyed.

Listening is the action of taking in the information that has been delivered. Listening is an essential part of the communication process that takes one's full attention and effort. It requires developing a psychological connection with the person doing the talking. It also requires a willingness to try and see things from the speaker's point of view and a desire to do so. At this point in the conversation, it is imperative that the listener refrain from passing judgment or making an evaluation of the message, and instead keep an open mind regarding it. Listening nonverbally is providing the speaker with one's entire physical attention or being aware of the speaker's nonverbal messages, whereas listening verbally entails paying attention to the words that are being spoken as well as the emotions that are being communicated. Verbal, nonverbal, and para-verbal listening are all important components of effective feedback collection for leaders, just as they are when passing on information to their followers.

Effective communicators convey their messages by taking into account the following considerations at the appropriate times:

1. The readability of the message (i.e., keep it straightforward and easy to understand).

2. The adequacy of the message, defined as the provision of sufficient data for accurate comprehension

3. The reliability of the message (ensuring that it is as accurate as the initial information).

4. The timing of the message (having it delivered at the right time and in the right place).

It is necessary for the communicator to ask for or solicit feedback from the listener to ensure that the message is being received and comprehended in order for there to be effective communication. In a nutshell, someone who is skilled in communication should also be skilled in the art of listening.

Additional helpful hints for strong communication skills are as follows:

1. Make sure you're making eye contact with the others in the room.

2. Have body awareness and project an air of self-assurance and persuasion.

3. Facial expressions and gestural patterns.

4. Express one's own opinions and ideas.

5. Get in the habit of using your communication skills effectively.

The process of effective communication involves participation from both parties. It requires both transmitting the message and engaging in active listening to receive feedback. It reflects both the speaker's and the listener's accountability in the situation. It is very easy to understand, and there is no tension present.

We frequently find ourselves in positions of leadership in a variety of settings and contexts. This includes leadership at the family level, as well as leadership at the organizational level and the national level. The desire to be a better leader comes easily to anyone who finds themselves in a position of authority, regardless of the level at which they find themselves. Despite this, there aren't too many people who have managed to be successful in this area. The inability of leaders to effectively communicate with their followers is one of the crucial tools that brings down the effectiveness of leadership.

The exchange of information between individuals is accomplished through a process known as communication. It was either expressive or receptive at the same time. The growth of both your professional and personal lives depends heavily on your ability to communicate clearly and fluently. It is also essential to the process of achieving greatness in leadership. Therefore, everyone who aspires to achieve leadership excellence should make it a priority to cultivate a mindset that prioritizes clear and effective communication, and they should make it a point to consistently improve on the art of leadership communication even before they achieve any degree of leadership position. By properly motivating and inspiring their people, good leaders are able to effectively communicate with them. In addition, the most successful businesses make communication both clear and efficient in order to foster a culture of discipline, accountability, and strategic alignment.

Communication is Comprised of Three Elements: the Verbal Message (the Words We Choose), the Para-Verbal Messages (How We Say the Words), and the Nonverbal Messages (Our Body Language). Messages that are lucid and to the point can be transmitted with the help of these three components. In addition to this, we rely on them to successfully receive and interpret the messages that are given to us. It is common for there to be confusion when the verbal component, for example, states "yes," but the non-verbal component reveals "no." In order to communicate well, one needs to coordinate the three components of communication such that they accurately depict the message that is being conveyed.

Listening is the action of taking in the information that has been delivered. Listening is an essential part of the communication process that takes one's full attention and effort. It requires developing a psychological connection with the person doing the talking. It also requires a willingness to try and see things from the speaker's point of view and a desire to do so. At this point in the conversation, it is imperative that the listener refrain from passing judgment or making an evaluation of the message, and instead keep an open mind regarding it. Listening nonverbally is providing the speaker with one's entire physical attention or being aware of the speaker's nonverbal messages, whereas listening verbally entails paying attention to the words that are being spoken as well as the emotions that are being communicated. Verbal, nonverbal, and para-verbal listening are all important components of effective feedback collection for leaders, just as they are when passing on information to their followers.

Effective communicators convey their messages by taking into account the following considerations at the appropriate times:

1. The readability of the message (i.e., keep it straightforward and easy to understand).

2. The adequacy of the message, defined as the provision of sufficient data for accurate comprehension

3. The reliability of the message (ensuring that it is as accurate as the initial information).

4. The timing of the message (having it delivered at the right time and in the right place).

It is necessary for the communicator to ask for or solicit feedback from the listener to ensure that the message is being received and comprehended in order for there to be effective communication. In a nutshell, someone who is skilled in communication should also be skilled in the art of listening.

Additional helpful hints for strong communication skills are as follows:

1. Make sure you're making eye contact with the others in the room.

2. Have body awareness and project an air of self-assurance and persuasion.

3. Facial expressions and gestural patterns.

4. Express one's own opinions and ideas.

5. Get in the habit of using your communication skills effectively.

The process of effective communication involves participation from both parties. It requires both transmitting the message and engaging in active listening to receive feedback. It reflects both the speaker's and the listener's accountability in the situation. It is very easy to understand, and there is no tension present.

PRACTICES RELATED TO LEADERSHIP

The information presented here is derived from Pages 13–22 of Posner and Kouzes's book, The Leadership Challenge.

A great number of authors, in an effort to assist people in gaining a deeper comprehension of the function of leadership, describe and define leadership. In general, authors have a tendency to advocate for a variety of leadership qualities or capabilities. When it comes to leadership, the focus may shift from one quality to another at times. Effective leadership can be characterized by a variety of behaviors, and Kouzes and Posner have identified a more comprehensive combination of these behaviors.

All five of these behaviors are essential for effective leadership, but some leaders may excel in one area more than others. These practices are modeling the way, inspiring a shared vision, challenging the process, enabling others to act, enabling others to act, and encouraging the heart. Modeling the way is the first practice.

1. Serve as an example. Take the lead and demonstrate proper behavior. It is essential to have a solid grasp of one's own personal values. The way we act needs to be consistent with the values we hold in common.

2. Inspire a vision that is shared by all. The vision is a collective aspiration or dream that will serve as the driving force behind the creation of the new future. Be a spark that ignites the flame of inspiration among those you lead by instilling in them a desire to make something happen and a shared vision for the future. In order to get other people on board with your plan, you should appeal to their goals that are similar to yours.

3. Put the procedure to the test. Those in leadership roles take risks to challenge the established order. Those who lead are the trailblazers. Those in leadership

positions are typically the first to try new things. Experiment and be willing to take risks by consistently achieving modest victories and gaining knowledge from your setbacks.

4. Open the door for others to take action. It is essential for a leader to have the ability to empower other people to take action. Foster collaboration by encouraging the pursuit of cooperative goals and fostering an atmosphere of trust. Help others become stronger by dividing power and discretion between you.

The Driven And Enthusiastic Leader

Imagine being part of a team where the person in charge isn't particularly enthusiastic about the work that they do. Because it is likely that all of the other members will also be unmotivated in this scenario, a great leader should be passionate about the goal as well as the process of getting there in order to inspire their followers.

When a person believes in something with every fiber of their being, they will experience the powerful emotion known as passion. A person's passion is what propels them to keep moving forward and committing themselves fully to their craft. If the leader of a team who is passionate about what they do shows that passion, the rest of the team will be motivated to feel the same way and will perform at a higher level.

It is indisputable that passion is something that can never be coaxed out of a person; consequently, each person should always have vision and mission statements that are articulated in a way that is both clear and compelling. These will help rekindle the fire of enthusiasm that served as the impetus for beginning the project in the first place. Someone who is committed to these statements, who lets this commitment reflect on performance, and who encourages the rest of the group to do the same thing is an example of someone who can be considered a passionate leader.

The Process of Becoming One:

Those who have the deepest level of dedication to the accomplishment of the team's objective are the most effective leaders. Use these techniques to reawaken the passion that lies dormant within you:

Achieve success through your own internal drive. Motivation can be either intrinsic or extrinsic, depending on what drives an individual. Someone who is learning to become a doctor because of the prestige that comes with the profession is an example of someone whose motivation to do something is extrinsic. Extrinsic motivation is when you are motivated to do something because of external reasons. On the other hand, intrinsic motivation is when you want to become a doctor because you are genuinely enthusiastic about assisting other people in need. Spend some time thinking about why you want to pursue something, and if you find that you are only motivated by things outside of yourself, make an effort to change your motivation so that it comes from within.

Maintain an open mind and heart for candid conversations. Allowing everyone on a team to talk about how they feel about a particular project is the most effective way to get people excited about working on that project. Before beginning the conversation, establish some clear ground rules, such as waiting for one person to finish speaking before turning the floor over to the other. The person who is currently holding the talking stick should not be interrupted while they are in the middle of expressing themselves, but they are required to hand it off to another member of the group after a certain amount of time has elapsed. Certain group leaders have a talking stick that is passed around the group.

Make your commitment public and clear. Your commitment will be etched in stone once you let everyone know that you are on board with the project one hundred percent, and it will encourage others to participate one hundred percent as well. People tend to become more committed and passionate once they are aware that all eyes are on them, so there is also a significant difference between keeping a promise to yourself and telling the world about it.

Because their work is something they genuinely care about, leaders who are driven by passion take complete delight in their work. Put yourself in a position to inspire others and bring about significant change by surrounding yourself with a group of people who share your level of enthusiasm and commitment.

Intellectually Communicate With One Another.

When it comes to speaking not just with your contemporaries but also with the members of your team, it is essential to communicate with them in a manner that shows respect and intelligence.

As a leader, one of your primary responsibilities should be to make sure that you are not the only one that learns and develops. You should assist your subordinates in learning how to get the most out of themselves as well as the circumstances in which they find themselves. When leaders inspire those they lead to be inventive and creative, it's possible that their followers will experience intellectual stimulation. It is crucial for you as a leader to instill confidence in the minds of your followers by convincing them that they are destined to achieve great things.

They have the potential to achieve great success if they put in a lot of effort, employ their intelligence, and are enthusiastic about what they are doing.

How to encourage creative thinking and intellectual curiosity:

Here are some simple strategies to prevent your followers from being uninspired and ensure that everyone stays on the cutting edge of change. The most disastrous scenario would be one in which neither your employees nor the firm itself would advance in any way.

Put forth difficult tasks. Make it possible for your followers to demonstrate their skills and abilities by setting up scenarios in which they can do so. This can be accomplished through various techniques, including training, seminars, and sessions focusing on team building. Together, you will be able to participate in activities such as playing games and coming up with new ideas.

Inquire about things. One issue that can arise with certain leaders is that they fail to consult their people by way of questioning. They are under the impression that they know everything, and as a result, nothing occurs. It is important to keep in mind that it is never inappropriate to seek the advice and assistance of others, even if you believe that you already have sufficient intelligence. Inquire about thoughts and comments from others. A good leader is someone who is able to take into consideration what others have to say and act accordingly.

cultivating a "I can do it" mentality and outlook. In the words of former President of the United States Barack Obama: "If they say we can't do it, we say, Yes We Can!" You have a responsibility to ensure that your workers are aware that, despite what others may think, the thing that matters most is that they believe they are capable of accomplishing great things. Maintain your agility, put in a lot of effort, and maintain a good mood while you're at work. Things are going to start looking up for all of you very soon.

Don't be so conformist about things. Do not be scared to attempt new things, and do not be afraid to push over the boundaries you have set for yourself. Imagine something completely different. If someone comes to you with a fantastic concept and you believe it has the potential to align with the values that your firm upholds, you should implement it. If someone suggests something to you that you haven't done before, don't be afraid to give it a shot. Even if a member of the team suggests something that is completely absurd, that does not mean that the idea cannot be successful. It is essential to have the ability to adapt easily in a changing environment. It's impossible to predict which ideas will be successful, but if you encourage your team to have the mindset that "no idea is a stupid idea," they'll feel more at ease voicing their opinions. If you continue to do the same things you always have, you will never be able to write your name into the annals of history. Do not let your fear prevent you from taking chances.

Create an environment that encourages innovative thinking at work. Give your followers the freedom to put whatever they want on their desks, as long as it is within reason and does not violate any laws, is unethical, or is in poor taste. Give them permission to decorate their workstations with anything they choose, including collages, vision boards, their favorite phrases, or anything else they can think of. A office that is brightly colored and lively is always preferable than one that is dreary and gray. They will view you as more than simply a boss, but rather an inspiration, and as a result, they will have a greater enthusiasm for the work that they do.

Take a look. Acquire the skill of paying attention to what is going on in the world around you. This can assist you in generating thoughts regarding what may be done and how you should conduct yourself moving forward. Recognize that change is an unavoidable reality. The only way that people will be able to connect with you and what you have to offer is if they believe that it will be beneficial to them in some manner. Show that you know what they want and need.

Don't overwork. Get out of the workplace after working hours, get an appropriate quantity of rest and the next day, you'll notice that you're ready and actually thrilled to work again. Don't allow your followers or yourself to get overworked. The brain doesn't work well this way. The brain's capability reduces as a person becomes overworked and inadequately rested. A creative mind is one that's able to get outside stimulation and enough rest.

Use Vision Boards. Vision boards can be corkboards where you can pin just about whatever that comes to mind—whether it your vision for the future, photographs of places you wish to go to or whatever it is you're experiencing today. You can also utilize the website Pinterest, if that's easier for you. Bottom line is that if you can see something, it can happen. The brain instinctively works toward accomplishing your dreams if you actually are excited by them and feel they are reachable.

And, know that it's necessary to learn something new each day. Never stop reading books, reading intriguing articles and getting to know diverse types of people. In this approach you will learn more about the world you live in.

The projection of oneself

People follow leaders because they have a unique attribute that is referred to as "force of personality." This is a famously difficult trait to define due to the fact that it is an abstract quality. On the other hand, one could characterise it. Let's give that a shot in this part of the chapter.

Having charisma.

A leader exudes a certain aura that compels others to follow in her footsteps. The word "charisma" is one way to describe this hidden quality that is within. The projection of an undefined and abstract characteristic by a person that has the result of drawing others to that person is what we mean when we talk about magnetic personality. There are many different factors that contribute to a person's level of charisma. It's possible that the individual possesses specific traits that distinguish him from other individuals, like complete honesty, for example. There are plenty of times when the majority of us are just partly honest or flat-out dishonest, despite the fact that we are generally trustworthy. Nevertheless, the quality that gives some leaders their appeal is complete and utter honesty. One such individual was the Prophet Mohammed, who was renowned for his unwavering integrity. As a result of this reputation, people felt comfortable entrusting him with their belongings when they went away on long-term business ventures, knowing that their valuables would be returned to them in the same condition in which they had left them when they returned. Because of their unwavering commitment to the welfare of their communities, certain political leaders exude an air of magnetic charm.

Hygiene of the person.

Maintaining a high level of personal hygiene is essential to successfully conveying an image of authority. A leader needs to have good personal hygiene. Take note of how spiritual leaders, who typically have a sizable following, constantly maintain a tidy appearance. Even if they have a beard, it is always well tamed and under control, regardless of how long it is. The age-old adage that "Cleanliness is next to Godliness" unquestionably contains elements of truth in it.

Body odour is the second most important aspect of personal hygiene, behind cleanliness. The smell of body odour is a natural byproduct of certain people's skin, and the factors that contribute to it can be rather varied, ranging from dietary practises to conditions that affect the skin. Others give off body odour as a result of the perspiration that their bodies produce; especially in tropical regions, sweat is a substantial emanation from the skin as a result of the heat and humidity of those conditions. Exertion of the muscles results in the production of sweat as well. Because so many people don't take the time to properly clean their bodies, they give off an unpleasant odour. Whatever the source may be, the effect of having a strong body odour is that it has a tendency to make other people avoid you.

Therefore, personal cleanliness is an essential social skill that plays a part in the development of a person's potential to become a leader. Take a shower every day to keep your personal hygiene in check. The hot water from the shower washes away the dirt and grime that has accumulated on the body, it helps to open the pores of the skin so that more oxygen can penetrate it, and it leaves one with a sensation of mental revitalization after taking a shower. It is important to wash one's hair on a regular basis in order to maintain it clean and free of dust and filth; this recommendation is directed specifically towards aspiring female leaders who wear their hair in long styles. It is recommended that male leaders who keep beards wash them frequently and, if they do not feel self-conscious about doing so, trim them so that they have a tidy appearance. It is highly recommended that a person always wear deodorant, regardless of the climate they live in, because the clean aroma of deodorant is both alluring and inviting to oneself as well as to other people.

Getting dressed.

Shakespeare once remarked, "The apparel oft proclaims the man," which means that people judge us based on the clothes that we wear. As a result, a leader ought to unquestionably make a fashion statement with the way he dresses.

Take note that we are using the word "style" in this context, and not the word "fashion." The current trend is what is referred to as fashion, and it is something that is constantly changing. There are a few styles that last for a considerable amount of time, but the vast majority of fashions are only fleeting. On the other hand, style is a personal statement that you make via the way you dress; it solely defines your individuality. You might take one or two elements from an ongoing fashion trend, but you should establish your own unique style—one that people will appreciate and try to emulate.

Shakespeare had a lot of insightful views to make about life in general, and one of those ideas was about the clothing that one should wear. Polonius advises his son Laertes in Shakespeare's play Hamlet, as Laertes is about to leave for France to further his education, "Costly thy habit as thy purse can buy, But not expressed in fancy; rich, not gaudy; For the apparel oft proclaims the man...."

In accordance with the guidance provided by Shakespeare, if you want to make a fashion statement, you do not need to dress in expensive garments; rather, you should select clothes that are within your price range. Your clothing should have an elegant and luxurious appearance, but should not be over the top. You have a flamboyant appearance, but it is not garish.

Your choice of attire should reflect the environment in which you will be wearing it. There are many different types of business attire, such as clothing for the office, dressing for a party with friends, and dressing for a company retreat.

We would like to offer you the following advice regarding your fashion sense: "Elegance."

There are six tests of one's willingness to submit to authority.

1. Those that are obedient are given instructions.

If you are a follower who is willing to submit to authority, then you will accept correction when it is given. You shall conduct yourself in a manner that is marked by reverence and a sense of modesty. It is possible for someone to point out your error to you. Keep in mind that in addition to being a leader, you are also a follower. You still have much to learn and grow in your relationship with Christ.

What do you say when someone brings a mistake to your attention and asks for your opinion on it? Do you put up a fight by defending yourself against others? Or do you want to cooperate and acknowledge the error? Your flesh has a tendency to speak up and say things like, "Who do you think you are to correct me? Do you believe that you are flawless? Who are you to point out my mistake? What gives you the authority to do that?

This in no way implies that you are required to submit to authority without question. There will be times when the correction that your authority offers is incorrect or goes in the wrong direction. But regardless of the circumstances, you should always respond by showing humility and being open to being corrected by them.

According to Proverbs 15:31, individuals who pay attention to constructive criticism are rewarded with wisdom. The verse states, "He who listens to a life-giving rebuke will be at home among the wise." Do not make the silly mistake of disregarding the correction or advice of others, particularly the advice of those who have more experience and more authority.

2. People who are submissive own up to their faults

If you are a follower, you will readily own the fact that you have erred. The education system of the world teaches that leaders never make mistakes, and if they do, they will not confess that they were wrong. However, this mindset only produces haughty leaders who are unable to defer to the authority of others. These leaders have the mindset that they are answerable to no one. As a Christian leader, you should have the ability to confess error and say, "I am sorry, I was wrong."

3. People who are willing to submit to authority do not "lord it over" other people (1 Peter 5:3)

The teachings that Jesus had to provide about being a servant have already been discussed. Because a servant respects authority, it is quite unlikely that he will mistreat the people who work for him. He won't demand or prescribe anything to you. He will not profit himself from his position in any way. If you adopt the mindset of a follower, you will have a far lesser risk of abusing your position of influence in the lives of other people. Because you are aware that you are also a follower, you will not attempt to dominate the situation. We are able to avoid "lording it over" other people when we submit.

4. People who submit to authority hold themselves accountable

If a leader does not accept that he is also a follower who is subject to the authority of another person, then it will be difficult for him to be held accountable. A submissive person does not put up resistance when it comes to submitting to authority and being held accountable.

A worker who is willing to submit to authority will gladly supply the supervisor with an accurate report. When a lady is subservient to her husband, she does not hesitate to tell him what she is doing or how she has spent the couple's money. A youth leader who is willing to submit to the authority of the senior pastor will not have any trouble reporting his plans to the pastor. It is not difficult for a subservient church member to approach the pastor and explain why she will not be in attendance at church on Sunday. A pastor who is willing to submit to the authority of his overseer or bishop will not feel any reluctance in reporting his activities to that authority. Every leader ought to answer to somebody for their actions.

Follow your dreams rather than the money.

To be a good leader, you need to have a clear idea of the goals you want to accomplish. I've lost count of the number of times I've witnessed somebody pursuing a promotion for the sole purpose of receiving a higher salary. You can't blame me if you think I'm mistaken about the significance of money in today's world, but it shouldn't be your primary motivation for seeking a promotion at work. Just for a moment, consider the reason behind your increased compensation. You get paid more than the standard amount because it is expected of you to perform duties that go beyond what is outlined in your job description. This is why you receive additional compensation.

The action you should do is to write down what your vision is. This can include objectives that you would like to accomplish while you are in your current position.

Put this objective into writing, along with a detailed action plan that includes stages that are simple to carry out. Make sure to write things down in the notebook that you always have on you. You don't have a notebook with you? Why shouldn't they?

The fifth lesson is that deeds are more persuasive than words.

This point is related to point number 2, and can go hand in hand with it. If you are pleased with the work that your employees have done, showing them your appreciation by providing them with time off or throwing a party for them is a great way to foster team building. This works a lot better than simply expressing gratitude, although expressing gratitude is already a good start in and of itself. Be the first person to pick up a brush when cleaning up, and others will follow your lead. This is similar to principle number two, in which your actions will speak more loudly than words.

It could be a good idea to have a celebration for your workers to demonstrate your gratitude for all of the effort they've put in, and you should also make a point of walking around the office and thanking your workers personally, as well as routinely praising them for their dedication to the task or job.

Take action and plan a get-together for your group.

Make an effort to express gratitude more often.

Flexibility in behaviour, but not in values, is point number six.

This is an essential one for your own personal wellbeing. It is not necessary for you to always act as the upbeat and positive leader. Take a step back in certain scenarios; go to lunch with some of the other employees; let your hair down at the company party; in short, shake things up a bit. On the other hand, behaviours are not the same as values. The way you conduct your life is directly correlated to your values, and the following is a list of the basic values that the British Army instilled in me:

Have some guts!

Control or self-control

Regard for one's fellow man

Having integrity

Loyalty

Commitment devoid of ego

As you can see, these are the standards that you should constantly hold yourself to, no matter what. That is to say, you are free to spend your time at the office party having a drink and having a good time with your coworkers because this kind of behaviour is acceptable. You have violated your own values if you have ever laughed at the expense of another person or gotten so drunk that you made a fool of yourself.

Take action and jot down the values mentioned above, or come up with your own set of values and save them in an easily accessible location in the office. Make an effort to remember them, and behave appropriately.

Have A Perfect Understanding Of Leadership Strategies

You need learn how to plan and strategize in order to be successful in this environment, which is constantly shifting and evolving. Why? Because if you don't, you won't really be able to be an effective leader, and it would be difficult to just watch your dreams evaporate into thin air if you don't do it.

Regrettably, not everyone is aware of the proper technique to strategize a situation. You will, however, be in the fortunate position of gaining knowledge about the myriad of methods by which you can empower not just yourself but also the others in your immediate environment through strategic planning. How to do it:

Recognise that you are not perfect in every way. Do not be the kind of person that goes through life pretending to be flawless even when everyone knows that this is not the case. If you are honest about your shortcomings and acknowledge the reality that there are still a great many things that could be done to improve your company, you are putting yourself in a position to take advantage of chances that are both larger and more rewarding. That is beneficial not only for you and your company, but also for the employees under your supervision. Always keep the expansion of your firm front and centre in your thoughts.

Determine what went wrong in the past, what is happening right now, and what could be done in the future to prevent this from happening again. It will be difficult for you to handle your line of work as well as the people who are around you if you limit your focus to just one time frame at a time. To avoid this difficulty, avoid focusing on just one time frame at a time. Find out what went wrong in the past or the mistakes that you have made in the past so that you will know what to do about it and so that over time, your company will grow to be the best that it can be. If you keep making the same mistakes, no one will trust you, which is bad not only for your business but also for your reputation. If you keep making the same mistakes, no one will trust you.

Concerning the state of your reputation, see to it that you maintain it. People are often saying that it is so difficult to develop a good reputation for oneself. In reality, it takes years, but all it takes to destroy it is a few seconds' worth of carelessness, or maybe even just one error. These days, people aren't very forgiving; occasionally, they believe that just because you're in a leadership position does not mean that you are immune to making mistakes. You must keep in mind that being in a position of leadership comes with a great deal of responsibility. Because of this, it is imperative that you demonstrate to others that you are worthy of the opportunities that have been presented to you and that you have the ability to disprove the naysayers. And more than just proving your detractors wrong, it's crucial to take care of your reputation for yourself and for your company. If people can see that you are trustworthy, then your firm will be more successful, and you'll have possibilities to take on bigger challenges in the future. This is why it's more important than ever to manage your reputation.

Surround yourself with exceptional people. When it comes to hiring new employees, especially those who will be reporting to you directly, you need to exercise extreme caution because you can't afford to have anyone but the most qualified professionals on your team. But try not to worry too much if things don't go as planned the first time around. There is no limit to the amount of improvement that can come from training these individuals. Activities and workshops geared towards the development of cohesive teams serve this purpose. What is important is that you all work towards improving things, and that you acknowledge there is a great deal more that each of you needs to learn. Instead of hiring people who are comfortable with what they already know, you should look for candidates who are willing to learn new things.

Never undervalue the importance of having accurate data. You have a responsibility to be abreast of what is occurring in your immediate environment, and you must be aware of the significance of monitoring news broadcasts. Do not be the kind of leader who is unconcerned with the people he influences or the customers he serves. It has nothing to do with being vain or arrogant; rather, it has everything to do with being aware of who you are able to assist and what you can do to expand your sphere of influence.

A knowledge of technology is essential, or at least the ability to adapt. Take a moment to ground yourself in reality and acknowledge that you can't possibly get by with simply pen and paper at your side. Learn how to use different kinds of new devices so that you can make your work easier, and also learn different ways to educate yourself. Learn about what's new in the industry, then apply what you've learned to your area of work. It is always necessary to know how to ride change and move with the flow of life rather than getting left behind, and one of the best ways to do this is to practise acceptance. If you have access to a sufficient quantity of resources, the load of work will be significantly reduced. Do your homework, and you'll be able to come up with some amazing ideas. Always be creative and original.

You, as a leader, have the ability to shape a prosperous future not only for yourself but also for your organisation if you engage in strategic planning.

How To Get Past Your Fear Of Having Panic Attacks

Attacks of panic are brought on by sudden bouts of anxiety that have an overpowering impact on both the body and the thoughts of the person experiencing them. It lasts for around ten minutes on average, and during that time it can be horrifying and is frequently feared. Many people who experience panic attacks are afraid to live their lives normally and avoid social settings and interactions because they have the perception that they are not in control of their bodies or their surroundings. It is possible for it to take an emotional toll on you, but if you are able to cultivate coping skills, it will be much simpler for you to manage the symptoms associated with it.

Attacks of panic can typically occur at any time and are characterised by a constellation of symptoms that can include uncomfortable physical constraints, troubling thoughts, and tense feelings. Sweating, shaking, and shortness of breath are some examples of the physical symptoms that can accompany anxiety, all of which can make the anxious thoughts, feelings, and sensations much worse and more acute. These unpleasant bodily feelings and symptoms can generate a great deal of unease and have an impact on your mental health. The majority of people who suffer from panic attacks have the sensation that they are having a heart attack. However, while their physical health may be fine, they may also have the sensation that they are losing their minds. Anxieties of all kinds can bring on a panic attack, which, in addition to potentially lasting for ten minutes, can also affect you in a variety of other ways for several hours after the attack has passed.

To conquer anxiety, you need to get over your anxieties, which includes any fear you might encounter that adds to your panic episodes. Once you do this, you will be able to overcome anxiety. If you are able to overcome things that are frightening or even intimidating, you will have less worry about confronting those things in the future. In spite of the fact that you may be prone to experiencing feelings of helplessness and being judged during this time, you should remind yourself that you are in control and that you have the ability to put an end to your panic attacks.

The following steps can be taken to accomplish this goal:

Get some training or education.

You will have a better understanding of your symptoms once you have gained clarity regarding the factors that are contributing not only to your panic attacks but also to your mental relationship with the fear of having panic attacks. You will realise that there is nothing physically wrong with you as a result of doing this, and that you are capable of overcoming the notion that there is something wrong with you. The more you learn about what's upsetting you or triggering your symptoms, the less likely you are to be afraid of your symptoms, and the better chance you'll have of getting through them.

Accepting that you will have panic attacks is the first step in modifying your reaction to the episodes.

If you can get a clear picture in your head of the symptoms you're experiencing, then you're already well on your way to recovery. You must now come to terms with the factors that are contributing to your panic attacks. It won't be easy because having to acknowledge and accept it can lead to additional feelings linked to anxiety and dread, but after you do that, you'll be able to recover from it. Acknowledging and accepting it can lead to more feelings associated to anxiety and fear. Taking into consideration the experiences you've had in the past, think about the anxious feelings you get and how on edge you get whenever you experience one of your symptoms. If you are able to alter the way that you think about panic attacks, you will discover that it is lot simpler to deal with them when they occur. When you have accomplished this, you will be able to modify your response to panic episodes. You will now have the option to deal with them in a positive manner as an alternative to merely responding to them as they act. In addition to this, whenever you feel as though you could be having an anxiety attack, you should give some thought to practising some relaxation techniques. This can be accomplished by activities such as yoga, practising mindfulness, or exercises that include deep breathing. If you alter the way in which you respond to your panic episodes, you will eventually be able to gain control over them through practise.

In a nutshell, you need to pay attention to:

Recognise the experiences, sensations, and symptoms of elevated anxiety that you are experiencing, and give yourself some time to think about what is going on with you.

acknowledge it - Instead of fighting against the symptoms of your panic attack, try to acknowledge that you are having one and make the conscious decision that you are not going to give it any control over you.

Respond actively - Rather of allowing your mind to take control of the situation, deliberately pick how you will react. You have the choice to think about how you will react before you react, and you can also choose to adjust your viewpoint on what is occurring to you. Consider it thoughtfully and keep in mind that you have complete control over the few minutes that it lasts.

allowing oneself to let go of the mistakes made by other individuals. Forgiveness is another aspect of life that is frequently misunderstood and undervalued, probably even more so than tranquility.After everything that they've done to me, how am I supposed to put their actions out of my mind? What exactly is it that you anticipate me to do, darling, other than lash out and let them have another go at it? It is not about condoning or excusing the behavior of the person you are forgiving; rather, it is about letting go of your resentment toward that behavior. When we engage in acts of vengeance, we link ourselves back to the source of our misery and misery to the source of our misery. We give our tormentor permission to cheat us out of more money once again. We give up a piece of ourselves every time we choose to channel our precious life energy into feelings of fury, contempt, retaliation, or counterattack.

You may still choose to cut that person out of your life, or you may continue with the claim; however, if you can do so calmly and without fear of retaliation, you have disavowed their influence over your passionate state. Simply take into account the fact that absolution operates in a dependable and harmless manner. We are given the opportunity to reclaim our creative energy, direct it toward more beneficial pursuits, go on with our lives, and continue with our own personal development when we are absolved of our sins. When we forgive others, we also grow as ourselves.

Always act with purpose, no matter what you're doing. According to a well-known proverb, "If by any chance you don't know where you need to go, any street will take you there." A lot of people, a lot of different people, are stuck in second gear as a result of passivity, which may be defined as the inability or unwillingness to settle on the major decisions in life and follow through on them. Passivity hinders people from moving forward. There are some people who really get caught up in this way of thinking, and as a result, they are unable to proceed healthily with the rest of their life. To grasp the concept of aim, one must first realize that settling on one thing to serve as the focal point of one's efforts necessitates sacrificing interest in a great number of other possibilities. Some people are unable to move because they are so terrified of making the wrong choice that the anxiety paralyzes them. Others might not be sure which options they'll have to give up because they're unsure what those options are.

Having said that, at the end of the day, not choosing is still a form of choice. One can get started with quite few options. Create them on purpose, take ownership of them, and center your attention on them. In this manner, things, for the most part, work out perfectly. Hold on to the more important ones on your decision rundown, and practice making the necessary adjustments to your behavior. You may find that it is easier to focus your consideration and energy on the things that genuinely matter in your life if you have a generally formulated proclamation of purpose to guide you, which is the conclusion you need to realize.

Prediction or anticipation. It has been brought to our attention by experts in the field of brain science that there is no such thing as success or failure in life. We manifest the lives we mentally prepare for ourselves. Although it sounds incredible, there is a significant amount of truth to what you've said there. The concepts of success and failure are merely verbal ideas; they refer to forms of evaluation that the human nature is bound to experience. Why would you want to make the event more emotional by stating things like "I failed" if you made the decision that you needed "A" but ended up getting "B" instead? Why not just mention that you required "A," but you received "B" instead? If you really want a "A," though, you're going to have to figure out a more sophisticated approach, right?

We are constantly "programming" conclusions into our lives, regardless of whether or not we are aware of this fact. There is definitely an element of luck involved in achieving one's goals, but anticipation and drive also play a significant role in this aspect of the equation. Your thought and your vitality will be centered on the outcomes you desire as a direct result of the clarity of your proposition and the quality of your desire. There is an old proverb that says, "Your vitality streams where your consideration goes."

You have earned the opportunity to achieve success in life. You have a propensity to advertise that you are questioning yourself or that you have lost your sense of reason to others when you are in either of these states. In addition, when you plainly have your eye on the ball, you have a tendency to express that to others as well. When given the opportunity to comment on dreams, professionals in the field of stress leaped at the chance to state the following: in order to make an exceptional dream a reality, you should first have an extraordinary dream.

Therefore, as you can see, there are a lot of things that need to be considered when you are looking at whether or not you need to focus on your spiritual life as part of your journey to success. One of the things that you need to consider is whether or not you believe in a higher power. It is not necessary stating that you need to be a part of any particular faith; rather, it is suggesting that you need to find peace and live out ideals that are generally part of a religious mindset or faith-based way of thinking, but don't necessarily have to be. When you are looking at the first pillar that will pull your life up toward success, you should take all of this into consideration.

To review, in order to gain the trust of the group as a whole, it is necessary to first earn the trust of each individual member. It can be fostered through being fair and objective, taking accountability of one's actions, and helping others achieve their goals.

Building trust with the people you manage directly and indirectly will give you the strength to lead and exert influence over those folks. It can also be accomplished by doing something as straightforward as following through.

Giving something back to the people you lead is an essential component of leadership. You open the door to mentorship opportunities by strengthening the trust competency in your organization. You mentor people to develop into more improved versions of themselves with your guidance. You will discover how to select the most suitable mentor for yourself as well as the most suitable individuals to serve in the role of mentors in the following chapter.

A quick review of mentoring: mentoring is a method to give back to the community while also passing on the knowledge and experience you have gained over your journey. You can also become mentees through this process, which will allow you to better comprehend new talents, technological advancements, and generational cultural differences.

You give the impression of having a sincere interest in, and dedication to, the people that we guide and mentor.

Throughout the duration of your coaching, make sure to offer constructive feedback and keep an open mind, be honest, and ask questions.

You are going to investigate the role of the coach in the following part. A coach helps someone on a route by leveraging the individual's knowledge and experience to define steps that can be taken to attain a goal or solve an issue, whereas a mentor guides an individual by sharing the mentor's previous experience and knowledge with the mentee.

www.ingramcontent.com/pod-product-compliance
Lightning Source LLC
Chambersburg PA
CBHW052147110526
44591CB00012B/1889